The Artist's Canvas

— Book Two —

A Collection of Inspirational Poems for the Soul

BETH SUNDBERG

THE ARTIST'S CANVAS: BOOK TWO
Published by Park River House
Grafton, North Dakota

Copyright ©2023 by Beth Sundberg. All rights reserved.

No part of this book may be reproduced in any form or by any mechanical means, including information storage and retrieval systems without permission in writing from the publisher/author, except by a reviewer who may quote passages in a review.

All images, logos, quotes, and trademarks included in this book are subject to use according to trademark and copyright laws of the United States of America.

Scripture quotations are from the Holy Bible, King James Version. (KJV)

ISBN: ISBN 979-8-9876252-3-1

POETRY / Inspirational & Religious

Cover and interior design by Heather Ward, Queenie Creations, copyright owned by Beth Sundberg
Editing by Joyce Beverly, MyStoryographer.com

All rights reserved by Beth Sundberg and Park River House

Printed in the United States of America.

Living Joyful

The memories that here abound
Were gathered places 'round and 'round.
And as you read the pages o'er
I hope you find that more and more...
A tear, a laugh, a sigh can do
Something to cheer you through and through.

May these pages remind you that life is for the living,
With joy, laughter, and unselfish giving.
To hold those you love close to your heart
Letting no anger and bitterness keep you apart...
May you be blest by the pages found here
As we are all blessed by God's unfailing care.

The Artist's Canvas

Praise 1

Creation
The Heart of the Rose 4
Northern Lights 5
Chameleons 5
He Gives Us Everything 6
I Knew God Was There 7
Spring Praise 7
A Rose's Story 8
Meditations on the Beach 9
The Sky People 10
Clouds 10
Fall Enchantment 11
Cactus Needles 12

Redeemed
Jesus Thought of Me 14
The Shepherd's Tears 15
Come Unto Me 16
Parched Living 18
The Father's Child 19
The Old Gray Bag 20
The Old Time Religion 22
God's Armor for Us 23
Sin's Fire 24
A Living Spark 26

I Thee Wed
The Carpenter's Plans 28
From Now and Forever 29
Together 29
Tom and Val 30
Love Is Like A Butterfly 31
Today Is Your Beginning 32
Dreams 33
Road of Life 34

Daily Living
Patience: To Wait on the Lord 36
Life's Ladder 37
The Essence of Love 38
Digging for Love 39
Lord Help Me Live 39
Sing A New Song 40
He Writes My Song 41
Our Circle of Protection 42
He's a Rock You Can Lean On 43
Thanks for a Smile to Share 44

Jesus Leading Line 45
Climb to Healing 46
I Love You My Child 47
A Thankful Heart 48
In Our Quiet Times 50

Family
Time's Misty Veil 52
The Welcoming Door 53
Suffer the Children to Come 54
My Best Friend 55
Mommy, I'm Scared 56
Thoughts on Babies 58
Our Brown-Eyed Bundle of Love 59
The Sights and Sounds of Summer 60
A School Day 62

Prayer
Vessels of Use with Feet of Clay 64
Trusting Him… For Little Things 65
Continue in Prayer 66
The Heart's Cry 67
Did You Think to Pray 68

Beauty from Ashes
Woven Threads 70
Ripples 71
From the Other Side of the Grave 72
The Silent Voice 73
Butterflies of Hope 74
The Transplanted Rose 75
The Call Button 76
Our Time 77
Empty Boots 78
Heaven's Glory Awaits 79
Wee Angel Babe 80
God's Child 81
The Hunter 82
Their Last Move 83
Between Two Heartbeats 84

Eternity
Time… and Eternity 86
Fleeting Moments 87
The Devil's Chains 88
One Last Call 90
Musings of a King 92
The Courtroom of the Ages 93
One Drop of Water 94
The Locked Door 96
In The Fog 97

The Ship of Grace 99

———————— ✻ ————————

Praise

When the eagle soars the thermals in majestic flight,
And you hear the wolf howling on a moonlit night.
The bugle call of the bull elk looking for his mate,
And the lonely cry of the loon flying over the lake.

Zephyr breezes that come sighing through the tall fir trees,
And sweet honeycomb nestled in a hive of bees.
The mountains reach toward the stars as if to say...
"This is the Altar of God; come kneel here and pray."

The rose sheds its sweetest fragrance alone in the night,
All the flowers in a mountain meadow shimmer in the sunlight.
And rivers ripple and chuckle over boulders in silvery spray.
The graceful deer and her fawn come to drink this way.

When every tree, bush, and blade is covered with hoar frost,
And the sun turns it to diamonds before it burns off.
The ocean waves curling up and over on the white sand...
Reflect the colors of each sunset painted by God's Hand.

The songbirds in the morning sing their paean of praise,
And gardens kissed by dew bask beneath the sun's warm rays.
A smile someone gives you as you pass them in the street,
And hymns that praise our maker when congregations meet.

All the earth does praise the Creator, whether song or bloom,
And the prayer of faith that's whispered lifts the dark of gloom...
So let's praise the God of Heaven for the gift of love, His Son.
May the joy and praise shine out and shed beams on everyone.

"Now unto the King Eternal, Immortal, Invisible,
the only wise God, be honor and glory
forever and forever. Amen"

— 1 Timothy 1:17 KJV

Creation

"I will speak of the glorious honour of thy majesty,
and of thy wondrous works."
— **Psalm 145:5 KJV**

The Heart of the Rose

Nestled within the velvety heart of the rose
Lies the essence distilled from the Father who knows
The fragrance of Love, wrapped in layers so fine,
Is only released in His perfect appointed time.

In the dark and cold of the winter sleep,
Its spark of life is hidden way down deep.
The stalks wither down to a moldering gray,
Seeming stunted and dead in the light of day.

When winter yields its grip and spring returns,
The glimmer of life within the rose still burns.
Then the warmth of the sun, a soft gentle rain,
Light breezes tickle o'er it and bring life again.

Then as the gardener turns the earth at its base,
And prunes the dead canes, leaving life in their place.
He waters it daily and fertilizes now and then,
Anxiously waiting for the blossoms again.

The Heavenly gardener lovingly watches His garden grow,
Clips here, trims there, shaping our lives just so.
And then like the rose, with the dross pruned out,
Our lives unfold and the fragrance of love wafts about.

The stiff canes of pride become pliable and soft,
And the sharp thorns of self are broken off.
The weeds of discontent, unthankfulness, envy, and lust,
Are rooted out and thrown on the garbage down in the dust.

And only as it yields itself to the pruning shears
Can the rose endure and survive for years.
So we, God's children, in His garden of Love,
Must yield ourselves wholly to the Master Gardener above.

Northern Lights

I woke up early this morning to a beautiful sight,
The skies all around me had a wonderful light.
An undulating wave of luminescent green...
Streaking and shimmering, then fading the scene.

The stars peeking through gave a silvery glow,
I stood arrested and awed, gazing from below.
I went from window to window, my awe untold...
And woke up the household, the scene to behold.

Oh, God of the Heavens, Creator of all things,
What awe and reverence this sight brings.
An unnatural light suspended in the sky...
And we question, "How does it happen?" and "Why?"

A phenomenon of the Northland, of cold and snow,
And the farther North you travel, the brighter the glow.
Brighter and lighter, the colors dance in the night...
Until each valley and hill glisten in their magical light.

Chameleons

Green, red, yellow, blue
I change my color to fit my mood...
My tail curls around the limb of a tree
While my sticky tongue snags a snack for me.

I live alone until it's time to mate...
Then I hope my colors, she'll appreciate.
My eyes can focus two directions at one time,
The better to see you; if it's my tree you climb!

He Gives Us Everything

Our wonderful, marvelous, merciful God,
Created the Heavens and earth, where we trod.
Mighty mountains and rivers, the great open seas,
The ant in the anthill, and birds in the trees.

Millions of stars in the Heavens above,
Pureness and beauty, in a gentle white dove.
The laughter of children, voices that sing,
He gives us the world... He gives everything.

Silvered heads bending, saints kneel to pray,
Thanking their Maker who leads them each day.
He gave His only Son for you and me,
Shedding crimson lifeblood on Calvary's tree.

He gave us the Bible, His own Holy Word,
Millions have heard it, and hearts have been stirred.
Blessings unnumbered, countless, yet more...
Never an end to what He has in store.

The world and its fullness, the Heavens above,
Hearts of parents and children, cleansed and filled with His love.
He's opened the way to the Mansions on High,
The redeemed of the ages He'll claim by and by.

I Knew God Was There

I saw a bird flying high in the sky,
I felt the sun shining warm on my cheek,
I heard a voice lift to Heaven in song,
And knew... God was there.

I sat by a brook flowing gently and slow,
I heard the music of the wind in the trees,
I saw a mother lovingly care for her child,
And knew... God was there.

I heard a soft whisper, so gentle and low
"Come child, together, we'll travel this road."
I listened, and yielded, then oh... such peace...
Yes... God was there.

Spring Praise

Spring winds blowing o'er the melting snow
Create ponds of water where the birds like to go...
Bathing the dust out of winter features
Grooming themselves for the mating weather.

Daffodils and tulips appear overnight.
The apple trees blooming are a beautiful sight...
Geese and ducks honking as they fly overhead,
And a songbird's choir serenades me in bed.

The musky sweet smell of awakening earth,
New babies frolicking, celebrating their birth.
All creation bursting forth with new life in spring...
Praising our great Creator... for everything.

A Rose's Story

A dewdrop trembled upon a rose,
And the rose tried to tell me all its woes.
All winter it was packed with snow and cold
"Now it's spring, and I feel so old.

My canes are gnarled, all ugly and brown,
And soon, I know, they'll need cutting down.
I will need some water, sun, and food...
And one day, I'll begin to grow so good!

My canes will grow tall, strong, and true.
I'll reach for the One who created me 'yond the blue.
And one summer morn, sparkling with dew,
Among my thorns, a bud will peek through."

Watered by dew, warmed by the sun,
The buds grow bigger... one by one.
Bursting with color, one day a beautiful rose...
Blooms, and its fragrance floats by my nose.

As each petal was shaped by the sun, wind, and rain
They whisper the story of God's love to man.
The downy softness of a baby's skin,
The rose a young man gives, his chosen one to win.

The bouquet a young husband brings to his first child's mother,
The rose a young child picks with his sister or brother.
Every rose tells a story, old yet so new,
Of the love in God's heart for me and you!

Meditations on the Beach

I sat on the beach watching waves foaming white,
And felt the salt spray as they crashed on the shore.
I went out to swim in their gentle, majestic might,
I watched a raging storm; they were gentle no more.

As I listened to their music, the waves crashing high,
And watched as the tide rolled on in...
I thought of the Trumpet of Ages drawing nigh,
And wondered, "Will I be ready, or lost out in sin?"

I saw the endless, relentless pull of the current,
And compared it to the lives of all men.
The ocean so vast... so deep...and so wide,
So too are the shadows of sin.

Though you walk in the shallows, the current draws you in deeper,
As the tide keeps on rolling forever, it seems.
It compels you to go a bit further each day,
Until you have lost all your pure hopes and dreams.

The ocean so mighty, turbulent., strong,
And it's tamed by the Master's one word...
So can the life full of sin be swept clean,
By repenting and claiming the Master as Lord.

Then as the current begins pulling you down,
You're anchored to the Rock, forever, on high.
You can stand 'midst the waves, though they buffet your soul,
Trusting... believing... your redemption is nigh.

Clouds

Flying high
Through the sky
Watching clouds floating by...

Wonder where
Those clouds prepare
Earth's rain to share.

Sunset glows
Red that shows
God's magnificence flows.

Written after flying west as the sun set

The Sky People

The sky people were playing in their cottony clouds,
Some boldly alone, some peeking from shrouds.
A truck climbed a hill above a small lake...
An island, blue water... no boats making a wake.

Several times rows of singers must have been practicing hymns,
Monkey people flying cloud to cloud on a whim.
Abe Lincoln showed up, Peter Pan was there too...
A thatched roof cottage appeared with a beautiful view.

An alligator, a horse, a bear eating a fish,
A car speeding down a hill looked like a death wish.
A seahorse, an Arizona butte, an angel lying down,
Resting from her labors just before sundown.

Then as the curtains were closing below
They lit up their playground with a beautiful glow...
Flashing on and off in the darkening atmosphere
So they all went to bed until their playground was clear.

Fall Enchantment

Wild geese honking as they wing by overhead,
And settle on open water as the sun sinks into bed.
Fall breezes that twirl colorful leaves off the trees...
And the buzzing hum of the honey bees.

Flowers that are waning, beginning to wither away...
Shelves full of produce preserved for a winter day.
Red apples turning into pie, crisp, and cider,
Pumpkin people twinkle beside the front porch glider.

Farmers rushing to get all the crops in the bin,
Scarecrows stare out in the twilight with a spooky grin.
Bonfires and poem fests around a blazing fire...
Singing in the gloaming, until your voices tire.

As the family gathers 'round the table laden with bounteous fare,
Thanking God in Heaven, for everyone who's there...
Missing those who've gone before, and left us here below,
Those three empty chairs leave a lonely shadow!

Tears come and go, just as harvests do...
And we thank God for every sunrise anew.
Laughter and song, family and friends...
A home in Heaven, when this trail ends.

Cactus Needles

In the desert, wind blowing all dusty and dry,
The sun burning hot in a cloudless blue sky.
Rattlesnake, coyote, and lizards all looking for shade,
Even the water in sheltered places evaporates and fades.

The cactus with its needles thrives in this dry land,
And behind its prickly covering, it stores the moisture God planned.
And many a man dying, thirsty, with no water in sight,
Can dig down past the spines and relieve his plight.

Like nectar from Heav'n, hidden deep in the heart...
It takes a man desperate, the prickly spines to part.
And the water that he searches and struggles to find,
Is more treasured than the richest gold ever mined.

So the soul bound by chains of the tempter's sin,
Digs a dry thirsty hole, blind and deafened by the din...
Until one day comes along a man with water so sweet,
That never fades away in the blistering heat.

So like the man dying in the desert who at last finds his well
In the barrel of the cactus that relieves his hell...
When he reaches to accept the water offered in love
He's tapped into the well that flows from Above.

Redeemed

"For God so loved the world, that he gave his only begotten Son, that whosoever believeth in him should not perish, but have everlasting life."
— *John 3:16 KJV*

Jesus Thought of Me

When Jesus sat at supper and knew that it was time,
That He must face the lonely garden, an uphill climb,
The cross and the nails, a traitor's kiss, a jostling crowd...
As they cried, "No mercy!" in voices harsh and loud.

Did His heart faint within standing in Pilate's hall?
When they led Him out to the scourger's wall?
As He hung by the chains while the whip whistled and snapped,
And cut the skin to ribbons on His legs and back?

Did He see them pick the thorns to fashion His crown?
Was His vision blurred from the blood trickling down?
Did He wish for a cloth to blot it out of His eyes,
And some wine to dull the pain that held Him like a vise?

As He staggered with His cross, did the splinters dig in?
Were His nerves stretched to breaking by the unholy din?
The shouts and the cries, the mocking laughter, and scorn...
The hunger and heat, His body weakened and torn.

Did He scream as the nails bit into His hands,
And the jolt the cross made as they dropped it to stand?
When the breeze hit His open wounds, did the pain make Him faint?
When He cried, "I thirst," the old sponge had a taint.

As His blood drained out and plopped into the sand
At the foot of the cross from His feet and His hands.
When the sky grew dark and soldiers gambled at His feet,
The Father turned away. The plan was complete!

When the weight of the sins of billions of souls
Pressed Him down to the depths of the fiery hole,
In the midst of that pain, He thought of you and me!
And He stayed on that cross so we all might see.

The place He's prepared in the Heaven's Above,
Where we finally may know the depths of His Love.
There we will thank Him again and again,
For His sacrifice of Love for sin sick souls of all men.

The Shepherd's Tears

The Shepherd's tears drip down one by one,
As He views each sinful thing we've done.
If we could just see the agony we put Him through,
His time on the cross. He lives anew!

Each time Satan tempts us with a besetting sin,
And we give in to his "wheedling" smallest whim...
The tears flow in streams on our Saviour's face,
We've wandered so far from that "cross of grace."

And the pain He bore, He bore in our place.
He saved us from even the smallest taste
Of deserving punishment and justice meted out,
Hell's flames engulfing us, no cooling water about.

Come kneel at the cross, when the tears flow on,
Let that cleansing stream heal you of all your wrongs.
And keep forever before you the vision of His tears,
Drop by drop streaming for you o'er all the years.

What love... oh what love... to give Himself to die,
And then we spurn it and His awesome cry...
"Father, forgive them, they know not what they do!"
Oh Lord, help us keep that vision in view.

Come Unto Me

When at night time alone I am pondering
All the events of the day...
In the stillness, I hear the Lord whispering,
"Have you done something for Me today?"
Then I think of my loved ones who are straying,
So far... on the cold mountains bare.
In my heart, I can hear Jesus asking,
"Have you tried to show them I care?"

Ah, brothers who are far from the Savior,
Bound tightly by Satan's black chains...
Of smoking, drinking, and riotous living,
With no thought whatever to the Master's great pain.
Oh, where will you be, wayward brothers of mine...
When all of a sudden shall come the end of all time?
Will you cry for the rocks and the mountains to fall,
To hide you from the face of the great Lord of all?

A trumpet will sound, skies roll back as a scroll,
Justice or mercy judged on the state of your soul.
Oh, eternal reckoning day for rich and poor,
Only God's children will enter Heaven's door.
Why won't you listen? A voice soft and low...
"Come unto Me, ye heavy laden... I'll lighten your load.
Your heart once so black, I will wash pure white,
And your soul will be filled with My holy light."

Oh, the blessings are many in God's Holy way...
There's peace and contentment, o'er a long trying day.
Trials and temptations, the world will allure,
But with God on your side, you can surely endure.
Oh, give to Jesus your heart and whole life,
Claim Him as Master amidst every strife.
The blessings of Heaven He'll pour out to you,
Then on judgment day, Heaven will be your view.

"Come unto Me, all ye that labor and are heavy laden, and I will give you rest."

— Matthew 11:28 KJV

Parched Living

He was walking his fields under the burning sun,
Watching the fruit on the vine dying, one by one.
The land blistering, cracking open, wider every day...
The sun's rays burning hotter, no clouds coming his way.

Sighing and wishing and praying for rain,
Searching endlessly the cloudless sky in vain.
The promise of his living fading away...
As he watches the fields bake into clay!

So the soul dabbling in sin hardens more and more,
Every day he goes further; the devil's winning the war.
And the soul that is parched, cracked, and broken within,
Can be filled with living water if he lets Jesus in.

The rain that He sends is from a sweet living well,
That fills us with love and alleviates our hell.
From so parched and broken, to love living inside...
Wide open to His water, with nothing to hide!

"Behold all souls are mine; as the soul of the father, so also the soul of the son is mine; the soul that sinneth, it shall die."

— *Ezekiel 18:4 KJV*

The Father's Child

Walking by an alley, a harsh voice rang out loud,
"I want that money!" she screamed, 'til the child was thoroughly cowed.
The woman was dirty, hair mussed and clothes torn,
She was looking for a fix. Her last one was yester morn.

The girl appeared hungry, skinny, and cold,
She looked up at the woman and couldn't break the hold
As the woman shook and screamed, and even hit.
The child looked desperate to get away from this fit.

I found the girl later, hunkered down by the bin,
Where trash is always thrown, she cowered therein.
As she sat with her arms covered over her head,
She quietly sobbed and waited with dread.

The look in her eyes is hopeless to see,
She knows from the abuse she will never be free.
But angels hover 'round her, unseen messengers of love
Sent to give her hope and courage from the Father above.

And He cries along with her as she suffers abuse,
In this dark world of hatred, which so many choose.
So Jesus' Arms of Love press her closer to Him,
'Cause He came to this world to overcome sin.

The Old Gray Bag

The man was tattered, shivering with cold,
No socks on his feet, shoes broken and old.
He carries a ragged and soiled gray bag
Everywhere he goes, his face lonely and sad.

He stays in an old van at the end of the alley,
Gets his clothes from the dumpster he digs through daily.
His beard has grown long, hair greasy and matted.
His hopes and dreams lie long forgotten and shattered.

Still, he defends his small place with a vicious snap,
And his death grip never loosens on the old gray bag.
Every day he carefully locks up 'his' space,
And timidly ventures out on the fringes of life's race.

Most days he shuffles down through the streets,
Looking for anything he can find to eat
Or trade for a bottle that he drowns memories in,
To dull the terrible hurt that is living within.

And the gnawing memories inside make him cranky and mean,
He doesn't care how he lives or how he is seen.
He's become lost in the shuffle of life and its knocks,
Not a penny to his name, not even clean socks.

But the angels watch over and care for him too,
Just as lovingly as they do for me and you.
'Cause Jesus suffered and died for him just as much
As those who have more, houses, possessions, and such.

And the Heavenly Father looks down on this suffering child,
As He cries along with him in this world gone wild.
His Father heart pleads, "Come, let me carry your load,
Then we'll walk on together up and down life's road."

And the old gray bag that he held on to so tight,
Is at last handed over, and his burden becomes light.
So the life that he lived is a thing of the past,
For he's found his burden bearer and joy that will last.

The Old Time Religion

There's a revival going on down at the old country church,
Where souls are saved from their hell-bound works.
The ministers preach the gospel night after night,
'Til sinners repent and turn from the world's false light.

That old-time religion that we love to hear,
Of a beautiful Heaven and a terrible hell to fear.
It makes us fairly tremble within our seats,
And we can almost feel that awful heat.

It makes your soul shrivel with shame, utterly lost,
And, oh you want to repent, whatever the cost.
Then as you listen and heed His tender call,
On the rock Christ Jesus, you'll brokenly fall.

His mercy and forgiveness are waiting for you,
As the scales fall from your eyes you'll see Heaven anew!
Reach out and touch Him with your body and soul,
Claim Him as Master of your Heavenly goal.

Peace and contentment, a ceasing from strife,
His Spirit to guide you in the decisions of life.
A love for all men and their lost guilty state,
Oh, tell that wonderful story before it's too late.

Thank God for revivals when once again we are stirred,
To renew our covenant with God and His word.
May we be humble, sincere, and true,
To the vows that we make on our knees to you.

That old-time religion of yesteryear,
May it still give us love and a Godly fear...
Down through the ages, today still rings as true,
As when Jesus taught the old story ever new.

God's Armor for Us

In the still watches of the night when you're counting sleep,
And you toss on your pillow and tangle the sheets...
The sins on your heart seem so deep and black,
Like the highest mountain: too high to cross to come back.

Fleeting moments of pleasure play on the screen of your mind,
Scrolling one by one. "Oh, I can't leave it all behind!"
The devil's imps chatter on; the roar and din ever grows
As they lure you on... you're full of heartache and woes.

In the midst of this clamor comes a still, quiet Voice,
"My child, I so love you. I gave you your choice.
I went to the cross. In great agony, I died.
My blood covers all of the sins you would hide.

Won't you let Me come in? I'll wash the sin stain away.
I'll teach you to love Me and to fervently pray.
My peace like a river will flow through your heart,
Come, take the first step... to life... a new start.

And the past with its blackness and sins blotted out,
Will release its hold on you. Come to Me... never doubt.
My shield of Faith and the Sword of the Spirit
Will be your armor if you'll only hear it."

Sin's Fire

In the forest reserve, where mountains are covered with trees,
And the sure-footed goat climbs to craggy heights in the breeze,
There's a home for the birds, the deer, elk, and moose,
The mighty grizzly bear, golden marmot, and Canadian goose.

Way up high on the hillside, where lightning strikes in a storm,
The sparks smolder in a tree that is dried out and forlorn.
The dead leaves piled around by the zephyr's song,
Are the fuel it needs that helps to push it along.

Building... flaring higher... bursting into flames hot and wild,
Ever growing ... moving faster... just so does an erring child.
Who begins to stray, hiding sins deep inside,
That burn a black swath in the heart you can't hide.

And when the fire has gone out, there are scars left behind,
And the memories they leave are a weight on the mind,
That our flesh tends to revel in, we live it o'er and o'er,
So we slide on toward the brink, facing hell's door.

But Jesus stands waiting, His scarred hands stretched out wide,
Beckoning for sinners, "Twas for you I died!
Come to Me, I'll forgive you. Don't believe Satan's lies,
Cast your burdens on My shoulders, My blood puts out Satan's fires."

And as we give our past into His sorrowing Hands,
Then we can trust our future in His loving, guiding Hands.
And the shame and guilt that go along with sin
Are forever forgotten when the victory He wins.

"Unto thee will I cry, O Lord my rock,
be not silent to me: lest, if thou be silent to me,
I become like them that go down into the pit.
The Lord is my strength and my shield,
my heart trusted in him, and I am helped.
Therefore my heart greatly rejoiceth;
and with my song will I praise him."

— **Psalms 28: 1, 7 KJV**

A Living Spark

Down in the depths of a smoldering pyre
Lives a spark, when fanned... becomes a burning fire.
And the whispering wind... directed by God's Hand...
Softly keeps blowing just as He planned.

Turning from blindness, to wonder... then sincere desire,
To know Him and find peace... from the dirt and mire.
And the winds of God just keep fanning that spark,
Until it burns brightly in a penitent sinner's heart.

Then the doors of our prison are opened wide,
And we're filled with the love of God inside.
Then we're free to love and free to sing,
His blood has covered everything.

And way down inside now burns a bright fire,
That compels us to tell others and never tire.
And whisper petitions to Jesus, "Please fan the spark
Hidden down deep in every struggling loved one's heart!"

I Thee Wed

"The voice of my beloved! behold, he cometh leaping upon the mountains, skipping upon the hills."

— **Song of Songs 2:8 KJV**

The Carpenter's Plans

By the blueprints the carpenter builds the walls,
Making sure to place the wood true and tall.
He builds a room where the cares of life wash away,
And another where his body is fueled for the day.

There's a room in his home where his family gathers,
To talk over the day and the things that matter.
And a room where each one has his own personal space,
There to meet the Lord as they kneel to pray.

He builds his home well, a haven from life's storms,
Where his family is safe, protected, and warm,
With a door thick and strong, and a roof overhead,
Comfortable chairs, and a soft downy bed.

He works hard on his home with precision and care,
And he's proud of his labor that he's done there.
So the Master Architect works on our lives,
Joining two hearts together as man and wife.

As we build on our marriage with Him as our guide,
He strengthens our weakness, as to Him we confide.
So keep building together with care for His plans,
Start each day with a prayer in the Carpenter's Hands.

And as you journey on, you'll find your home strong and true,
Stand together 'gainst the world with Heaven your view.
Learn to be patient, treat each other always with love...
And your home will become a taste of Heaven above!

From Now and Forever

From now and forever
As husband and wife,
Hold hands, kneel to pray
In your everyday life...

"I'm sorry," and "forgive me"
Always clears the air,
And makes a happy,
Contented home to share!

Together

A flash of her eyes, he glimpsed through the crowd,
And the smile that she gave him broke like sunshine through clouds.
His shoulders look wide enough to carry the load,
So today they are starting as one down life's road.

Like a candle flame flickering and wavering in the wind,
That soon sputters out unless cared for and trimmed.
Protecting each other from the currents of sin,
That batter a marriage, trying to destroy from within.

Together they'll learn to trust their Heavenly guide,
To lead them on paths where He walks by their side.
And the dreams they dream will be guided by His love,
His blessings shower down from His storehouse above.

Tom and Val

Soft, misty dreaming, I see a maiden's eyes,
She's building a little home up to the skies.
She's dreamin' of pleasant little dinners for two,
Laundry and canning and cleaning to do.

A young man's heart reflects in his eyes,
As he too dreams of winning his prize.
That special lady enthroned in his heart,
He is dreaming of a home with a Heavenly start.

Long miles apart, two prayers ascend to the Throne,
Asking God's will in the start of a home.
God drew them together; in Wisconsin, they met,
And the fire that God laid was brilliantly lit.

And so they have dreamed and planned and worked,
And not one detail for this day was shirked.
Now today they have joined their two hands as one,
Through fair or stormy weather, through shade and sun.

Through sickness and health, in joy or sorrow,
God bless them with faith, hope, and prayer for tomorrow.
May they daily overlook all the little frustrations,
That would drive them apart if it's left up to Satan.

God bless them with happiness, laughter, and tears,
An open door of hospitality to all through the years.
Bless them with patience, and understanding hearts,
In fervent prayer for others, may they do their part.

Maybe Tom will need help with a cantankerous cow,
And Val is too short to reach that jar somehow.
Give them soft laughter and a song or two,
When sometimes, in the evening, the horizon seems blue.

Pray together and sing that song
Even though it seems things are going wrong.
A prayer and a song turn everything light,
'Cause God blesses those who live in His sight.

Love Is Like A Butterfly

Love is like a butterfly's wings,
Flashing iridescent in the sun.
As two separate hearts
Begin blending into one.

God bless you this day
And all your days through
Which He, in His great love,
Has allotted to you.

Today Is Your Beginning

Today you are starting a life that is new,
Solemnized by the words to each other, "I do."
The future looks bright, you have love and each other,
But always remember the One who brought you together.
He has guarded you both on your pathway through life
As two separate beings... Now you're one... Man and Wife.

Take Christ as the head of your home built for two,
May each day start with Heaven's hope in your view.
Make your devotions a place where others love to join in,
As together you serve the One who reigns over sin.
May your home be a place of hospitality and prayer
Where others are blest by the joy that you share.

The road will get rocky and the valleys be deep.
The climb up the mountain will often seem too steep.
Take one day at a time with its laughter and tears,
Soon the days will become months, and the months become years.
Then someday you'll look back o'er that long winding trail
And realize your love has grown stronger through each gale.

So today looking forward to your future together,
May God bless you richly through all kinds of weather.
Through poverty or wealth, in joy or sorrow,
May you look forth each day with hope to tomorrow.
Teach your children the Bible, help them learn of God's Love...
Then rich blessings will be showered from Heaven above.

Dreams

From the piney woods to the treeless plain,
Came a young man looking for his fortune and fame.
Driving his Ford pickup truck, often far too fast,
Neighbors wonder where he's tearing to, as he breezes past.

He loves crawfish and truffles; despises vinegar salad...
Sometimes by his driving, we wonder if his eye prescription is valid.
But through the long years, he has lived and learned.
And now he's found something, for which his heart yearned...

A young lady to love him; I hear she's a good cook...
Maybe oft in the evening, he'll find her with a songbook.
And after they share their cozy dinner for two,
Their dreams in the gloaming will have a bright rosy hue.

Maybe those dreams will include the patter of tiny feet,
A couple or three would make their home complete.
And always above, around, and throughout...
Swirls the Love of the Father, who brought this about.

Every breath we breathe, every beat of our hearts...
All the love that we share is a gift He imparts...
And it lightens the load we carry each day,
As together we travel, toward Heaven's golden highway.

For Courtney and Bailey

Road of Life

Long are the years you have traveled
Down this lonely road we call life.
And a bit of your heart must have ached
Each time a friend became someone's wife.

But now finally has come the long awaited day
When you've been asked to come away...
To the far-off mountains with your red-haired man
And his seven chillen. That's quite an array.

From flat North Dakota to the Pennsylvania mountains
From secretary... to wife and Mother...
When God asks us to change, sometimes it's real big
But the blessings will be like no other.

Sunrises, sunsets, and rainbows' glow will be brighter
With someone you love to share...
And mundane chores like laundry and dishes
Will fly by on wings of thankful prayer.

And when you're sitting 'round the fire at night
Looking up at the big full moon...
Remember those you love and left behind
Are watching the same big moon.

Daily Living

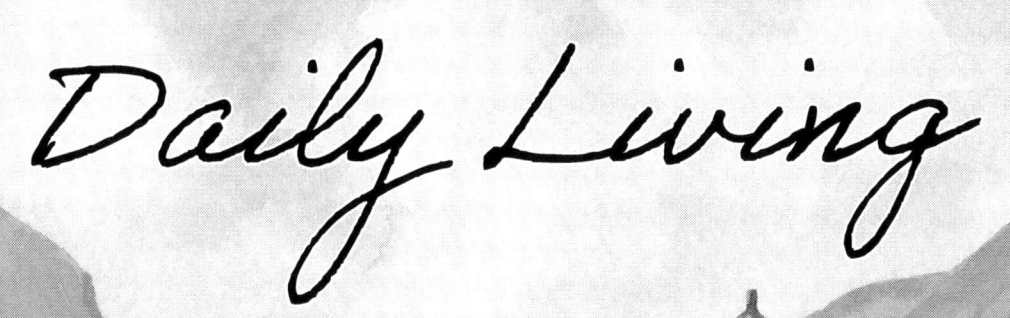

"He is like a man which built an house, and digged deep, and laid the foundation on a rock: and when the flood arose, the stream beat vehemently upon that house, and could not shake it: for it was founded upon a rock."

— Luke 6:48 KJV

Patience:
To Wait on the Lord

To patiently wait in the midst of the storm,
When our livelihood's threatened, we feel lost and forlorn.
And worry and depression set in our house of cares,
As we take our burdens back from the place of prayer.

To be cheerful and happy when the clouds hang low,
And teardrops continue to ebb and flow.
When the crops are still, standing tall in the field,
All summer we've worked hoping for a good yield.

But the clouds hang on – almost every day –
And my patience has gotten up and walked away.
"Where's your faith?" someone asks as I grumble and complain.
How will we pay our bills without the check from the grain?

Faith: an act of my will. I choose to believe in our God
Who takes care of us each day wherever we trod.
Our faith grows each moment we put our trust in Him,
E'en though Satan tries to keep our vision dim.

With an unthankful heart to our heavenly Father,
We let clouds of discontent fill us, 'stead of prayer at His altar.
Our calm patience to wait on the Lord is gone,
Along with our love, joy, and cheerful song.

When I catch a vision of my ugly spirit within,
And ask Him for grace, there is victory to win.
Then though the clouds are still hanging there,
My heart can be calm as I kneel in prayer.

I can patiently wait until the sun shines through,
Realizing that God controls the weather too.

"Wait on the Lord: Be of good courage,
and he shall strengthen thine heart:
wait I say, on the Lord."

— **Psalms 27:14 KJV**

Life's Ladder

Splintered, rungs broken... tied together with twine...
Weathered, unsteady, this life's ladder we climb.
Young and invincible, we start out alone...
Never dreaming that we might be accident prone.

As our foot slips off a rung, a hand catches a splinter...
Holding tight we struggle on, fear, making us shiver.
If we reach way up, there's a hand reaching down
Waiting to lift us at our first desperate sound.

Stretching out of sight, into the infinite blue,
New vistas beckon us, up toward the ethereal view.
And when we step off into that Heavenly land...
We'll join those who are waiting at the Savior's right hand.

The Essence of Love

Love is the essence of things not seen,
It's channeled from Heaven to each human being.
If the oceans were ink and you'd fill the sky above...
'Twould not be sufficient to tell of God's Love.

Love, that is true love, never grows old,
'Tis a blessing to have and a joy to behold.
There's always a way you can tell if God's Love
Is filling your heart like a gentle, pure dove.

It shines forth as a smile or kind word on the way...
To some poor, careworn traveler you meet every day.
It's a cup of cold water or a job that's well done,
Or the flower garden weeded out in the hot sun.

It's the love of a Mother for her babe, just born,
And the kind words of Father on a cold, cloudy morn.
It's a brother or sister who love to tease,
Then when troubled comes to you, "Can you forgive me, please?"

Love is the reason that we can be saved,
That Jesus, our atonement... His lifeblood gave.
Love comes from Heaven to you and me...
As soft as a whisper on the wings of a breeze.

Digging for Love

Like a well driller, boring down deep,
On and on down, to the water seep.
And as they dig deeper, more debris is cast out...
Until at last pure water is breached with a shout.

So must we dig and renounce pride, self, and sin,
Take Jesus our Saviour, gaining sweet peace within.
And as our heart, cleansed of sin, opens wide...
The love of our Father fills up the inside.

And the deeper we go, the more love that it holds,
Like a well flowing over, running free and bold.
Transparent as glass, imperfections are seen...
Yet strained out by the love in the Master's screen.

Lord Help Me Live

Lord help me live from day to day,
In such a kind and helpful way,
That others 'round me all will see,
The beauty and Love of your Spirit in me.

May I be brave in the face of each test;
For I know in my heart it is for my best.
Let me lean on Your strength to get through every trial,
And to learn through the darkness to keep a bright smile.

Sing A New Song

Dear God up in Heaven
As you look down upon me,
I wonder, just what
In my heart do you see?
Do You see selfish pride
In my walk or my talk?
Or an unwilling spirit,
For things You ask me, do I balk?
Do You see some rebellion
Hidden down deep?
Instead of giving all,
There's something I want to keep?

I'm sorry, dear Father,
I'm so prone to stray.
But what can I do
When I want my own way?
Won't You please wash me,
Cleanse me from sin?
My heart is all Yours,
Make Your home now within.
Then as You look down
From Your throne up above,
You will see a heart cleansed,
And filled with Your Love.

Oh, grant unto me courage
When the road seems too steep,
And when I pass through valleys
Dark and deep.
I will hold on to Your Hand
And by faith walk along...
When I've passed through the trial
I will sing a new song.
Oh, thank you, Father
For this gift of Your Love...
That is wafted so gently
From Your storehouse above.

He Writes My Song

I hold a pen as He writes my song
And if I allow myself, I sing along.
Maybe sometimes I'm a step off key...
But He still writes the song, just for me.

The chords I sing are full of joy each day,
Unless I choose to live life in a selfish way.
Then the chords jangle discordantly,
As I try to pen my song for me.

But when I only hold the pen,
And allow the song to be written by Him...
The chords ring true and pure and sweet
And vibrate through the air from the Master's feet.

As I sing my song to the Master's tune,
It can lift the dark of someone's gloom.
May our songs ring out every day...
As we pass through this world on life's highway.

Our Circle of Protection

When the tempter besets us on every side
With doubts and fears, ugly self and pride...
Turmoil and unrest, critical thoughts within,
Jealousy, gossip, lust of the world and its sin.

Like a windy spring day, he buffets us sore,
Until it seems like he tries to ooze into our pores.
From one direction, then another he tries to get in
If we crack the door carelessly, soon the threshold he wins.

Stronger and stronger, the arrows fly thick and fast,
Some land on target, some zip on past.
In the midst of the storm, there's a haven of love,
Our Heaven-sent armor from our Savior above.

A barrier thick and strong as we kneel in prayer,
However hard Satan tries, he can never enter there.
Our prayer beams to Heaven on a direct line,
And our Savior responds, with protection just in time.

With love so big, so deep, and wide,
The devil can only run away and hide.
For a time we are safe from his slavering hate...
While we pray to our Father, he must stand by and wait.

And wait... and wait... and his hatred grows.
His demons rage in fury as they try for our souls.
But our shield of faith and the shining sword,
Continue to protect us, as promised in God's Word.

He's a Rock You Can Lean On

When troubles press in and all around,
And the problems of life begin to confound,
Where do you go in your trouble and tears...
To the One who can quiet and calm all fears?

He's a rock and a mountain you can climb,
A still quiet lake, reflecting peace sublime.
He's a baby's downy skin or first tiny smile...
An older child's hug and "I'll see ya, after while!"

A cup of cold water to someone on the way,
Warm clean clothes at the end of the day.
A quiet peace stealing into your heart...
When you've placed your faith in Him, you've done your part.

Simple little things: a smile across the room,
A glance together at the big full moon,
Rockin' a baby in the middle of the night...
As you pray to Him to give you insight.

Wisdom for life's problems comes from Above,
As we ask for His guidance and give him our love.
His blessings unnumbered each and every day...
Coming more and more as we live His way.

Thanks for a Smile to Share

Can I smile when my heart is heavy,
When I'm burdened and troubled with care?
When the trials of the day press upon me,
And leave me too tired for prayer?
When it seems like old Satan is trying
With all of his powers to leave my soul crying...
Oh God, what's the use? I am near to despair.
Where shall I go in my sorrow and care?

Can I smile when my friends
Turn their backs on me...
And leave me alone in distress
Just when I need their help most?
When the sun on the horizon
Grows dimmer each minute,
As the trials in my soul
Encompass everything in it;

Oh, God up in Heaven
Please help me to see
All the beauty around me
In the flowers and trees.
The reflection of Heaven
In some kind person's smile
Or the touch of Your Spirit
As I pass through the trial.

Help me to smile, though the day be so drear,
My soul tired and weary, and my eyes filled with tears.
For when I've come thru this trial,
I'll be thankful Your joy has made it worthwhile.
Yes, the fight was tremendous, but You're always right there
With Your Spirit for comfort to my desperate prayer.
You're the soft, soothing Peace flowing into my heart,
As each day, I endeavor from the world to depart.

Thank you, Heavenly Father,
For the gift of your love,
And all the blessings and power
You send from Above.
By Your grace, each victory I've won
Is through the death and resurrection of Your Son.
So thank you for the smile that you give me each day,
To share with some traveler, I meet on life's way.

Jesus Leading Line

Can I smile when my heart is heavy,
Down in a dungeon as black as night,
I fear to take a step without a light.
But the builder so carefully thought of it all...
And He chiseled a groove in the side of the wall.

And the groove is just deep enough for my finger
To use as a guide so I can go on and not linger.
In the stygian dark, afraid of what's ahead...
I can climb toward the light because I am led.

By the light of the cross, Jesus chiseled His prints
Into every heart who's received Him since.
And the groove that He carves into your heart and mine...
Forgiveness, Peace, and Love will make our life shine.

And He continues to groom and trim us with care.
To His Father, He intercedes for us daily in prayer.
So our faith ever grows as we follow His line...
Until He leads us safe home at the end of our time.

Climb to Healing

A vessel, cracked and broken, was thrown in the gutter...
As I passed by in the street, it seemed to mutter.
"I'm no good at all, I'm dirty and soiled,
My handle is cracked, and my pouring spout spoiled.

I'll just hide in the dust, down here for a while,
Maybe no one will see me on this side of the pile.
The potter created me, beautiful, shiny, and clean,
Now my shine is all gone, I feel ugly and mean.

I tried to tell someone I was grossly misused,
But they were sure I was trying to get others abused.
Oh, why can't they hear me? I'm crying for help...
But my cry goes unheaded! My heartache unfelt."

But the Master Potter has heard my cry.
And He reaches out to me. I don't know why.
He sent me a friend to pull me out of the pile,
And sometimes at night, I dream awhile.

My dream is a vision... the Master Potter's house,
And I hear strains of a song before I rouse.
The Potter loves his creation, He's reminding me again.
Though I'm still lost in my pile because of others' sin.

But now with some help, I'm beginning to climb,
From the depths of the pile, one day at a time.
One step forward, and sometimes, two steps back,
'Cause memories grip me strong, like a weighted pack.

All the anger and guilt that were a part of my life,
Are beginning to release their stronghold inside.
I'm learning the Master Potter has my good always in mind,
As He carefully mends the broken pieces He finds,

And someday... I'll look down from the top of the pile,
Maybe then I'll understand what made the climb worthwhile.
May He bless all who've traveled with me, this journey to healing,
And send help to each vessel still broken and weeping.

I Love You My Child

I love you my child, oh I love you my child...

My Father woke me today saying, "I love you my child!"
Oh, what a shelter from life's storms, dark and wild.
He's my Saviour and protector, my guide as I travel...
And He washes me when I'm covered with dirt and gravel.

When the wild winds blow, and the hills get steep,
And the devil keeps trying to lull me to sleep,
He wakes me and loves me, gives me water to drink...
Living water that saves me from hell's fiery brink.

He's my comfort in sorrow, my calm in the storm,
My food on the table and clothes to keep warm.
He corrects me when wrong; His blood covers my sin...
He gives me a song when together the victory we win.

I love you my child; I gave to you life,
And I want you to love Me amidst toil and strife.
Learn to trust Me in the things life throws your way...
Thank Me for loving you at the end of the day.

A Thankful Heart

There was a storm that passed over during the night.
In the morn, I awoke to the sound of birds' delight.
I wondered what they were saying to the Heavens Above...
Their home looked quite ragged, yet they sang with such love.

So I thanked my maker for the gift of our home,
For food in our pantry, even the dog has a bone.
Clothes to keep us all warm, a vehicle to drive...
That He woke me this morning: "I'm still alive!"

Choose to treasure your family, your children, and friends.
One day there'll be a morning when someone's summons He'll send.
Thank Him for clean air, for the flowers that bloom...
The trees in the forest that form His cathedral room.

For sunrise and sunset that He paints with such care...
Many an artist keeps trying, but can never compare.
Unseen and unheard, our hearts keep pumping away,
Eighty times every minute without prompting each day.

This human heart's blood can give life to a stricken brother,
But only God's grace fills hearts with love for each other.
So thank Him for that love, and ask Him for more...
Enough to help someone, their faith to restore.

You can't out-give Him you know; just keep trying, you'll see.
Gratitude grows like a river that runs to the sea.
Its waves are far-reaching, gathering others in...
As it tumbles and flows through this world filled with sin.

So instead of a grouch, fill your life with thanks living,
With laughter and joy, and a heart full of giving.
Love as if no one has ever loved before...
Sing, so it carries to Heaven's door!

GRATITUDE

Three qualities belong in a definition of gratitude.

The first is **appreciation**.
You recognize that something is valuable to you
which has nothing to do with its monetary worth.

The second is that gratitude is **free**.
Gratefulness is the key to a happy life that we hold in our hands.
If we are not grateful, then no matter how much we have,
we will not be happy because we will always want
to have something else or something more.

Humility is also a key to having a grateful heart.
We realize everything we have, comes from God.
We could not even take one breath,
without His gift of the breath of life.

In Our Quiet Times

In the quiet time in your mind,
Where do you go?
Where flowers bloom, the sun shines warm,
And breezes gently blow...
Or the potholed, boulder-strewn path
Where clouds always hang low?

The rough cloudy way
Is the way of despair.
Unforgiveness, unthankful, critical
Thoughts are found there,
Fueled by the devil's imps
Whispered in your ear.

And the grooves get deeper, deeper
As our mind spins on...
Ever drifting downward
Toward the devil's spawn.
Where fog clouds the vision
And our peace is soon gone.

The higher sunlit way
Climbs up, narrow and steep...
Our minds fixed on Jesus
We must always keep.
Then the devil stands away
Gnashing his teeth.

Family

"And let the peace of God rule in your hearts,
to the which also ye are called in one body; and be ye thankful."
– *Colossians 3:15 KJV*

Time's Misty Veil

There's some gnarled old trees on the side of the hill,
Where once used to be a home, now it's silent and still.
And the house is weathered down to a silvery gray,
Though the walls seem to echo sounds of children at play.

The rope swing hangs crooked, tattered, and frayed,
And the sandbox timbers are all rotted away.
A hoe lies discarded amidst long scattered seeds,
The barn door creaks in the silence, almost hidden by weeds.

A few stray pieces of hay drift down from the mow,
Left from the time the barn sheltered the cows.
An old dried-up harness hangs forlorn on the wall.
There's a battered gray bucket in a corner stall.

The pump in the garden is rusted and old,
And in the granary wild animals have been bold.
The springhouse by the creek where they used to keep butter,
Has a wild rose canopy; there bees and butterflies flutter.

And the windmill turning with a creak and a groan,
Hasn't seen the grease can since the children left home.
The mailbox is bashed in at the end of the lane,
Half a sunset reflected in a broken windowpane.

Precious memories linger, flitting about the old place,
Bringing smiles, and some teardrops, that slip down our face.
And the love that we shared in our old childhood home,
Still brings us back from wherever we roam.

The Welcoming Door

There's a little old house behind a white picket fence,
Roses climbing up the wall, so thick and dense.
The windows all sparkle in the bright sun...
And the swing from the old tree in the garden looks fun.

The sandbox in the backyard still has some old toys,
That welcomes the neighborhood girls and boys.
There's a bike in the garage, alongside a wagon and trike...
An old hoe for the garden, along with boots for a hike.

Some low wooden rockers on the porch in plain view,
Where people passing by can old friendships renew,
With a glass of cold tea, some cookies or cake...
That Grandma always serves on an antique plate.

And the door to that welcoming place by the road,
Is the threshold others pass for help carrying their load.
All it takes is one knock and it swings open wide...
Loving welcome lies within as you step inside.

Suffer the Children to Come

Nestled beneath a mother's heart,
God made a place for babes to start.
Life here on earth, sent from above,
To fill us with wonder and lots of love.

Petal soft skin, a dimple or two,
Fine downy hair, maybe a smile for you.
Ten fingers and toes... like Mom or Dad?
God has given to us this fine little lad.

You counted the months before he was born,
Then suddenly he was here on a gorgeous May morn.
Now you'll count years of his life with you,
And teach him to keep Jesus and Heaven's hope in view.

Diapers and pacifiers, blankets, rattles, and toys,
Trucks, tractors, barns, and animals make happy little boys.
A sandbox, a swing... skinned knees now and then,
"Mama's kiss makes it better," he'll say, with a grin.

Cuddled together in the rocking chair at night,
Reading Bible stories and singing lullabies, slow and quiet.
As his eyes blink slower and slower at the sand man's tug,
Then he's tucked into bed with a prayer and a hug.

And Mother lingers o'er his bed and watches him sleep,
Sighs a prayer for his future and the path for his feet.
Precious little lamb, lent to you, from Above,
Teach him obedience and patience... but most of all Love.

"But Jesus said, Suffer the children,
and forbid them not, to come unto me:
for such is the kingdom of heaven."

— Matthew 19:14 KJV

My Best Friend

"To my best friend, my Dad," the inscription ran
On the special knife I received from a man...
The son I once cradled and rocked and loved,
Taught to ride a bike and play ball with a glove.

I sat with him in the hospital when he broke his leg,
And tried to teach him to hang the tools on a peg.
When the tears trickled down and he shuddered with fear...
I took him up in my arms where I dried each tear.

And I told him I loved him, as I kissed his hot cheek...
As I felt this gift given, so awesome it made me weak.
I thanked the God from whom I received this gift,
And prayed he'd understand when I made mistakes and slipped.

I wonder if he understands when all I do is cry,
As I think of the mistakes, and all the questions, "Why?"
But He surrounds me with His love, filling all my empty spaces...
And I feel His loving Hands wipe the tears from my face.

I know my best friend is my Heavenly Father above,
And I pray my sons can see a small portion of His love
In the life I live and how I love them too...
"O God give me grace for a glimpse of Heaven and You!"

Mommy, I'm Scared

"Mommy, I'm scared," my little girl said,
Of the dark, the wind, and "What's under my bed?"
Just a little one, I can take on my lap...
Soothe, dry her tears; kisses and hugs before her nap.

We cuddle them close, give them baths, feed them bread,
And how many stories over the years we have read.
We take them to church and soon they start school...
Then so soon, there are ball games and the local pool.

Bike rides and camping, staying with friends overnight,
And when they walk back through our door, it's a wonderful sight!
They grow up so fast; now it's our turn to be scared...
Never knowing what challenge they'll accept when dared.

And one day amidst life's duties, they don't come home!
We frantically search, praying, while someone stays by the phone.
Their bike left in the ditch by the side of the road...
A lonely shoe found down by the railroad.

Now at each sound in the night our heart jerks with fear,
As sleepless we lie, searching... in our minds, everywhere.
Is she lying frightened? Is she warm? Is she fed?
Or tossed alone somewhere... crumpled and dead?

I need someone to hold me! To kiss me good night.
To soothe this ghastly terror; tell me it will be alright!
Dear God send your angels to cradle our little one...
I know you see her, even though evil seems to have won.

May angels whisper in her ear of Your love.
Let her see Jesus coming through the stars above.
Oh Lord, keep us from blaming You, for allowing this terrible thing.
Help us remember that the devil still wants to be king.

You've given each soul the freedom of choice,
And the wolf that we feed is the one which gives voice.
One is full of anger, jealousy, selfishness, and greed...
The other is love, joy, forgiveness, and peace. Which wolf do you feed?

Thoughts on Babies

A baby's a mystery, ever old, yet so new,
They come bundled up, in pink or blue.
They're so precious and tiny; so innocent... pure,
And soon have us wrapped around their heart's door.

A baby depends on its Mother each day,
To tend its each need and teach it life's way.
And as it grows older, each day it will be
A reflection of its mother's daily company.

A baby that's healthy, sweet, and content
Responds to cheerful loving and prayers that are sent.
Love – sees a mother through life's ups and downs,
Dirty diapers and flu, even the frowns,

A love that never diminishes with age,
That grows stronger and stronger, each day in life's page.
A love that is sure, when there's training to do,
To ask the Lord first, "Will You see me through?"

A baby is something you never ignore,
They get into cupboards and closets, eager to explore.
They're a natural result of woman's love for man,
A God-given gift, part of His plan.

What a beautiful picture to see a baby that's happy,
Just to bounce on the knees of its mother and daddy.
In a home filled with laughter, song, and love,
And prayerful obedience to the God above.

Oh, Father in Heaven, bless these parents and child,
As they travel life together, bless them with Your smile.
May they rise each new morning and kneel to pray,
Thanking You for Your Love and blessings this day.
Amen.

Our Brown-Eyed Bundle of Love

Big brown eyes shining with joy
At the piece of candy or a brand new toy.
A pink bow of a mouth, smiling so sweet,
And the steady pattering of inquisitive feet.

A lisping little voice softly asking for a drink,
Tiny little hands want to help at the sink.
Her sweet baby face framed in blond curls
Is the loveliest sight God placed in this world.

She depends on us for all her daily care,
And closes her eyes when it's time for prayer.
She follows me around saying, "Rock me to sleep."
Our hearts throb with love, ever more deep.

"Hold me," and "What's that?" are her favorite words,
And she loves to be shown the kittens and birds.
She's a precious little bundle of innocent joy.
Who would ever think they'd rather have a boy?

God bless little girls with their tousled curls,
As they grow into women in this troubled world.
Bless them with character, courage, and love,
May they always place their faith in God above.

*For all parents, grandparents,
uncles and aunts of little girls*

The Sights and Sounds of Summer

The sights and sounds of summer excite the mind,
To thoughts of happy friendships' ties that bind.
A time to live a little bit slower,
To draw close to God in His earthly bower.

To see a rose-colored sun in the early morn,
Watch the lightning and thunder of a summer storm.
Hear the robins chirping, a family playing croquet,
A fire-lit picnic at the end of the day.

A motor boat speeding across the lake,
And the wonderful smell of chocolate cake.
A lawn mower's roar, a child's trilling laugh,
And the hungry bawl of a newborn calf.

Hamburgers sizzling on the barbeque grill,
And flower pots blooming on the window sill.
Little boys fishing, and catching frogs,
Blue smoke rising from a burning log.

Crickets' chorus in the still summer night,
And jet planes flying out of sight.
A rooster's crow, clothes flapping on the line,
The muted cry of a puppy's whine.

Tractors churning up the rich black loam,
A lonely feeling when you're gone from home.
The smell of new-mown hay, sounds of dishes clattering,
Small children's feet and their inquisitive pattering.

A swimmer's splash, friends joining in song,
Softly voiced prayers to keep us strong.
A rocker creaking, a clear rippling brook,
And time to relax with a favorite book.

An all-day rain in the middle of summer,
Telephone calls to the local plumber.
Fireworks exploding in the darkening sky,
And the mosquitoes' buzzing brings a long-suffering sigh.

Young people driving up and down Main Street,
And the local Dairy Queen is the place to eat.
The Stars and Stripes waving o'er the Land of the Free,
An afternoon baseball game is where boys like to be.

Quiet evening walks down a narrow country lane,
Golden sunsets reflected in my window pane.
Neighbors dropping in for a few minutes to chat,
The door is always open with a welcome mat.

The full moon shining, a blooming potato field,
The clink of jars in a canner, nighttime stars revealed.
A six o'clock whistle blowing, a cooing mourning dove,
June wedding bells ringing for young couples in love.

Homemade ice cream, fresh strawberry pie,
The scent of flowers in the air, and a blue, blue sky.
New friends and old, laughter and song...
These are sights and sounds that, to summer, belong.

A School Day

The doors bang open, and in they come,
Their first day of school – oh how fun!
Spelling and math and reading to do,
Learning to get along with others too.

We start each day with "good morning" to each one,
Devotions are next, with prayer and song.
Not a ritual, but real: asking for help from Above
For teacher and children to treat each other with love.

Lessons come next, Teacher helping one then another,
And we must learn to be patient, respecting each other.
Recess is next: many games are played together.
Good sportsmanship is taught in all kinds of weather.

Whose turn to sit by Teacher at lunchtime today?
Can we take turns or do things have to be done "my" way?
This one is bossy... that one is shy...
That boy over there always asks "why?"

Storytime comes next. We can color while Teacher reads.
Now it's time for those with special needs.
And through the day many times teacher sighs.
To discipline is so hard... do they understand why?

The bell is ringing; the school day is done.
What battles were fought... and how many won?
The teachers sit down to reflect on the day.
Students happily go home to run and play.

We know the old standards of discipline with love
And respectful obedience are gifts from Above.

Prayer

"The LORD hath heard my supplication;
the LORD will receive my prayer."

— *Psalm 6:9 KJV*

Vessels of Use with Feet of Clay

This vessel of clay that houses my soul,
Would hold me back from reaching my goal.
'Twould make me falter, stumbling along,
Losing my way and happy song.

Exploring the side roads along the way,
For Satan's imps, I am easy prey.
Bad habits, attitudes, and unkind thoughts;
Many and hard are the battles I've fought.

Temptations beset me on every side,
Criticism, selfishness, and ugly pride,
Pop up pretty often, and my feet of clay
Keep me mired in the mud 'til I kneel and pray.

On angel's wings, my prayer takes flight,
From this house of clay to the realms of Light.
And there it finds a place to rest,
Beneath our Saviour's spear riven breast.

And then that prayer the Father hears,
As His Son intercedes for me with tears...
Those angel's wings bring back to me,
An answer drifting gently on the breeze.

Then this vessel of clay is lifted up,
And filled with an overflowing cup.
Full of His love and cheerful song,
Willing to help my fellowman along.

And tho' I falter and fail again,
I know He's there to forgive my sin.
He lifts me up from the miry clay,
As long as I ask for His help each day.

Dear Lord, as You look down on this vessel and see
How I struggle to keep my eyes on Thee...
Cover me with the crimson flow from Your side,
Blotting all my sins written in the book of life.
Amen

Trusting Him... For Little Things

Just a little thing you say?
Too small for God to care?
He cares much more than you can know,
He even counts your hair.

Each little thing along life's way,
The bitter and the sweet,
He's longing for you to trust to Him,
He'll make your life complete.

Continue in Prayer

The pathway to Heaven is narrow and steep.
Our eyes focused on Jesus, we must always keep.
And often read His word, and pray to Him...
Lest our spiritual vision begins to grow dim.

Satan walks beside us, and whispers in our ear,
And soon we begin to doubt and fear.
Our eyes turn down the side roads of life...
And the things of the world begin to entice.

Our eyes off Jesus, we begin to stumble and fall.
The cares and allurements of this life become our all.
One disobedience leads to another along the way...
And soon we forget to kneel and pray.

"Oh, I'd never do that, how terrible that he fell,"
Someone said as they sat on their lofty pedestal.
Except for God's grace, it could be you caught in sin...
Satan tries his best, every Christian to win.

Oh come down from your heights and help your fallen brother,
Show him the love that God gives us for each other.
Lift his faltering feet with a smile and a hug...
Spend some time on your knees; speak to our God above.

Pray, pray for loved ones who have strayed away,
Send love and encouraging words in a letter today.
Sing some songs to someone battling despair...
And remember to always continue in prayer.

Pray for a love for the fallen and lost...
Pray to keep oil in your lamp, whatever the cost.
Remember God made us and gave us each other,
And love... not a name, is what makes us a brother.

The Heart's Cry

Some straying son's mother on tired knees bending,
Humbly in prayer at the close of day,
Talking to God with pleadings ascending,
For her lost wayward loved one, long gone astray.

Someone's kind father with lines on his face
With broad shoulders bent, heartsick and sore,
Is praying and crying in some secret place...
"My child, oh have mercy. Call him once more."

So many brothers and sisters are longing,
Praying that someone will soon come back home.
Softly, tears falling, we hear them all sighing...
"Call them, oh call them, no longer to roam."

Oh, wandering lost one, far out in sin,
Many are praying and watching for you,
Each prayer ascending, your soul to win...
And find your salvation, Heaven's hope to renew.

For families who have a loved one straying

Did You Think to Pray

Did you think to pray this morning
E'er you left to start the day?
Did you ask your God for guidance,
Grace, and power on the way?
Can you feel His strength uphold you
When the tempter tries his wiles...
And he wants to make the journey
Seem just like a million miles?

Are you weary of the struggle
When the heated fight is on?
Does it seem as though the losses
Count up more than those you've won?
Is your courage sinking lower
'Til it seems you're in a pit
With the walls 'round you growing taller
As you mire down in it?

Just look up toward the sunrise
As a prayer breathes past your lips...
And the warrior angels rally
Coming swift, before you slip.
There they join the battle with you,
Chasing off the evil horde...
As your prayers ascend to Heaven
Like an incense to the Lord.

Beauty from Ashes

"Blessed be God, even the Father of our Lord Jesus Christ, the Father of mercies, and the God of all comfort; Who comforteth us in all our tribulation, that we may be able to comfort them which are in any trouble, by the comfort wherewith we ourselves are comforted of God."

— 2 Corinthians 1:3,4 KJV

Woven Threads

When the death Angel comes for someone we love,
And they hear that call sent from above.
The gossamer strands of life that are woven,
Become thinly stretched, then suddenly are broken.

We're left with our hearts so bleeding and sore,
Wishing we could follow them through that door.
Yet life must go on... and in our dark night,
It seems as if God sends a small light.

He sends a rainbow's beam to arch over our heads,
We dream we hear angels while lying in bed.
So faint... so pure... so golden in tones,
Are the songs they sing, welcoming someone home.

Oh, wait upon the Lord; He'll renew your strength,
And the hills before you, you'll climb at length.
On the wings of an eagle, you'll lift up high,
The doors of Heaven will draw you nigh.

Oh, let Him lift you up into the realms of light,
And dispel the despair and sorrowing night.
Then rainbows, with prisms of brilliant beams,
Will pierce the dark with sunshiny gleams.

And the strands of life that once were broken,
With a different pattern will again be woven.
Into a fabric, strong and lovely to see,
For God adds the threads missed by you and me.

Ripples

There are questions we ask as we mourn and cry
And God weeps along with us as we ask, "Why?"
No answers really come, just a sense of His love...
And it drifts down gently from His storehouse above.

When someone takes a life, it's not part of His plan!
His choice is living, filled with service to man.
So cry when you need to! He cries along with you...
Then He sends you a beautiful sunset to view.

In the stillness of the night, tell Him your fears; ask Him, "Why?"
His angels hover 'round you, they hear your every sigh.
Our parents and families, teachers, preachers, and friends...
Are your angels on earth; listening ears, they will lend.

May you allow God to calm all your questions and distress.
Filled with His love and mercy, your soul will be blessed.
And like ripples on the water, may that love spread around...
Until others ask you where this love can be found.

"To appoint unto them that mourn in Zion,
to give unto them beauty for ashes, the oil of joy for
mourning, the garment of praise for the spirit of heaviness;
that they might be called trees of righteousness, the planting
of the LORD, that he might be glorified."

— Isaiah 61:3 KJV

From the Other Side of the Grave

We run too and fro, doctoring here and there,
And quickly buy a wig when cancer treatment takes our hair.
We try a nerve relaxer when we feel a little stressed...
And still, we fret and worry, forgetting how we're blessed.

We hang on by our fingertips to every breath of life,
In this dark world of sorrow, turmoil, and strife.
Every twinge of pain, we find a medication for...
Putting off the day when we're called to death's door.

But from the other side of the grave,
They look on and wonder why this life we so crave.
Saints gone before gather 'round the white throne...
Singing and waiting for loved ones coming home.

Our mansion is ready, the table set for us there,
Angels standing by to show us to our chair.
The great Heavenly choir is ready for another voice...
All Heaven awaits the Master's next choice.

He calls whom He will, His timetable alone,
And He sends a new babe as He calls someone home.
So let's hold this life loosely as we await our call...
To join the redeemed in the great gilded hall.

Inspired by some thoughts about the joy
that must be in Heaven when someone is coming home

The Silent Voice

This water that washes down over our eyes...
Droplets that follow your earthly demise.
You left us too soon, leaving three empty chairs.
Now, all we have left are loving memories we share.

All your trials here are over, your work on earth is done,
You followed God's call into the setting sun.
We'll miss your low chuckle, your ready helping hand,
Your home and food shared with many a needy child or friend.

Now your voice has gone silent, your home shrouded and still.
You'll lie over in the churchyard; we can visit you at will.
We trust you, our loved ones, into the loving arms of God,
As we lay you all to rest beneath the sod.

Butterflies of Hope

When morning breaks on your darkest day...
I'm afraid it will be 'cause I was called away.
You'll reach for me as you turn your head
And touch that empty pillow at the head of the bed.

The sun will seem darker; the birds cease to sing...
An empty pall will drape over everything.
You'll ask God, "Why," and "What shall I do
With these little ones you gave to us two?"

My vacant chair at the table; clothes piled on the floor,
The kitchen is empty, we need a run to the store.
Meals to cook; a pile of jeans to mend,
Bible stories to read, and a garden to tend.

Who will teach our girls how to comb their hair,
Or how to sew a modest dress to wear?
The boys to be gentlemen, how they should treat a wife...
So they have a happy home, free from strife.

You'll turn to whisper sweet words just for my ear,
As we used to do in yesteryears!
The memories will scroll across the screen of your mind...
Bringing tears, sometimes a laugh, for all I left behind.

And as the days drag on, slowly fading away,
Arises a butterfly of hope to fill your heart someday...
There'll be another God will place in your heart
And life will be sunnier, right from the start.

And the hollow left behind when I crossed the divide
Will be filled with joy at love's incoming tide.
As that tide washes in and covers your dry land...
You'll be led by His path, clearly marked in the sand.

The Transplanted Rose

As the caretaker walks through the garden each day,
Snipping the weeds and smoothing the clay,
He tends to the watering, and loosens the soil here and there.
I know if we listen, we'll hear a soft prayer.

He whispers again His story of Love as He works,
Clipping and straightening each flower's quirks.
Some have grown old, thick and gnarly with age,
Others, supple and strong in their youthful stage.

As He moves along, touching with infinite care,
Those tender plants He's transplanting there,
He chooses the most beautiful blossoms each day,
To come grace His table and walk Heaven's way.

This beautiful rose that He's asked you to share
Will be waiting to greet you when you get over there.
Its fragrance grows sweeter in your memory o'er time,
And you'll long to join him in those beauties sublime.

The Call Button

Such a sweet little lady lying helpless in bed,
Blindly reaching to find a button that slid down the side instead...
The blankets are rumpled, the pillows askew,
And a dingy wall with some ductwork, her only view.

She's lived a long life full of laughter and some tears,
Now the flame is burned out. She's flown to a higher sphere...
But while here below when there were trials and tests,
There was someone she called on, putting fears to rest.

And the drunkard with a bottle, the pill-popping crowd,
The murderers and thieves, scoffers shouting aloud...
Popular singers with their lyrics, stirring base desires,
Cheating homewreckers and their children caught in the crossfire.

The liars and rapists, prisons are bursting with them,
And homeless souls struggle to find home again!
Atheists spouting discord, immorality, jealousy, and greed,
And just one call on Heaven's line would fill every need.

Just one touch of that button, our finger shaky and cold,
And sometimes before we call, He's sent the answer tenfold.
He anxiously waits for each child's distinctive ring,
And His angels wait silent, ready His answer to bring.

And the little lady dying in her bed,
With her grandsons beside her, struggled and said,
"Do you hear?" Angelic voices from a celestial realm
Sang her from earth to her Heavenly home.

Our Time

When our time here on earth is beginning to wane,
Sometimes we're asked to endure much pain.
And these earthly ties that bind us here,
God slowly weakens, preparing us for a different sphere.

And our loved ones walk with us through the deep vale,
Watching as this house of clay becomes weak and frail...
Every tear shed heals a place in our hearts,
Assuring us we'll still be loved and missed when we're apart.

Every special smile, small visits here and there...
Softly voiced songs, countless whispered prayers.
As our valley gets deeper and darker and long,
We can almost hear a faint Heavenly song.

And then one day God says "It's enough.
It's time to come home to the mansions above!"
Then you'll fly... fly away on an angel's wing,
To the golden streets and join in songs to the King.

And to all those left behind on this earthly shore,
"I'll be waiting for you when you come to that door.
Remember me in the children's smiles...
Be thankful... I'm free, now walking these Heavenly aisles."

Empty Boots

I saw some empty boots sitting in the street
Waiting for some worker's cold and tired feet.
He's working hard to feed his family well,
And those worn, empty boots have a story to tell.

I see a mother standing lonely at her door,
Wishing for a glimpse of a son who's gone to war.
And she lingers at the mailbox, hoping it's today...
The letter that he promised will finally come her way.

She sends his favorite cookies, new socks, and underwear
Praying God will keep him safely in His care.
A fleeting vision crosses the screen inside her eyes,
Empty boots and rifle... his friends saying their goodbyes.

I see some little children, playing in the rain,
Splashing through the puddles that form along the lane.
Rain boots, mud pies, and Legos evolve into ball games and cars...
Young people 'round a bonfire, singing 'neath the stars.

And all the empty boots each one has left behind
Sing a song of memory in their loved ones' minds.
Laughter, songs, loving hugs, tears, and more...
Once filled those boots someone left beside the door.

Heaven's Glory Awaits

I've crossed o'er the river into Heaven's bright land,
Now I'm quietly resting at the Savior's right hand.
I've gone on before, but I'm waiting for you...
Heaven's a beautiful place I want you to see, too.

All you that I left on the earthly shore,
Don't be turned away when you come to that door...
The pleasures of that world don't begin to compare,
With the beauty and glory awaiting you here.

Don't make me look in vain for your beloved face,
Even though there are no tears in this wonderful place...
I want our family to be all together again,
In this beautiful home where Eternity begins.

For an uncle

Wee Angel Babe

Your tiny angel was lent you for a while,
Just anticipating her appearance gave you both a smile.
She came to you so perfect, ten fingers and toes,
A sweet rosebud mouth and a tiny button nose.

And the angels sang as God called her away,
Welcoming her back to Heaven to sing and play.
And someday not long in the future, I know
You'll see her again when He calls you from below.

In between, your wee babe will be cared for and loved
By the angels of Heaven in the realms above.
Just picture her now in the arms of the Father
As He cuddles and loves your precious daughter.

Imagine her smiling and kicking her feet,
So happy to be in His arms where life is complete.
And the Father, in His mercy, reaches down from Above,
As He holds her, He comforts your lonely hearts with His Love.

So let Him hold closely your babe and you,
And the hope in your hearts He will surely renew.
Every minute of the day when the hurt is so big,
Just reach up for the comfort He is waiting to give.

God's Child

A tender bud that bloomed today,
God has seen fit to call away.
He lent him to you for a while...
To give you joy and make you smile.

His busy hands and pattering feet,
He made your family so complete.
Don't cry and groan and wish him here...
God transplanted him to a different sphere.

He'll bloom and grow in the Heavens above,
As he waits for you in the realms of love,
Where grass and flowers grow abundantly fair...
And most of all, Jesus is there.

The gates are of pearl, the streets of gold,
And angels sing sweetly, hymns of old.
God gave him to you for a little while...
Now He summoned him home to be His child.

The road goes ahead for many long miles,
And you'll need a song and a friendly smile.
May God comfort and bless your lonely hearts...,
With the peace and contentment His Spirit imparts.

The Hunter

'Twas a happy time when he loaded his gun,
Down in the bottoms, watching his coon dog run...
Looking for wild hogs, 'possums, or coon,
By the silvery light of a big full moon.

Tramping through the woods with his dog named Head,
Flushing squirrels and rabbits, splashing through the stream bed.
Campfires by the river where he caught his fish...
Cleaned and sizzling in the skillet, the best camping dish.

Watching the fog drift 'round the cypress knees,
And the sunrise glisten on the dew-laden trees.
God's cathedral, hushed and waiting for a whispered prayer...
As your soul is renewed in quiet meditation there.

May the God of the rivers and woods that he loved
Surround you, his family, with peace from Above...
I pray the angels will carry you through this dark time
'Til you hear distant echoes of a heavenly chime.

Memories shared grow sweeter as you learn and grow.
And now you walk this new path God's given, your family to know.
And though his chair sits empty and we don't understand...
There's a better home waiting in the promised land.

Their Last Move

They moved to their new home a week ago today,
They received a call and answered right away.
"Hello? Yes, God, we're here and ready to go,
No rushing or packing or dresses to sew."

They crossed o'er the River and eons of time,
And stepped on the shore of beauties sublime.
Now they wait 'neath the altar with saints gone before,
Grandpas, Dennis and Wayne... and so many more.

Did the angels add another board in the table for you?
Does your mansion up there have a beautiful view?
Are you singing today in the Heavenly choir,
Where your voices never grow hoarse or tire?

Now, though our tears flow and we'll miss them so much,
How can we question our Savior's touch?
For He touched all of us here, left to await our call...
And what will you answer when He calls for your soul?

Will you answer: "Yes Father, I'm ready to go."
Or will you face demons and imps, fire leaping from below?
Oh, make your decision this hour, this minute...
Before judgment falls on your soul and what's in it.

*In memory of a dear uncle and aunt
killed in a head-on car collision*

Between Two Heartbeats

Between two heartbeats, God called you away.
From the wheel of your truck, you stepped Heaven's way.
His hand stretched out over the River of Time
Beckoning you come into Heaven's joys sublime.

Did you see the angels as they guided you along?
Was your soul filled with the singing of the Heavenly throng?
Were Uncle Harlin and the boys there to greet you at the gate...
Did they take you to the table, where your name sits by a plate?

Your heartbeat lives on in your children's lives,
And the helpmeet God gave you, your beautiful wife.
These ties that bound you to this world's toil...
God released you to soar upward from this mortal coil.

Can you see us down here, struggling on in our grief?
I know you'd tell us to let our crying be brief.
To miss you, but live joyfully... to make many friends...
Waiting 'til God calls us upward at our trail's end.

Eternity

"Verily, verily, I say unto you, He that heareth my word, and believeth on him that sent me, hath everlasting life, and shall not come into condemnation; but is passed from death unto life."

— *John 5:24 KJV*

Time... and Eternity

Life is made up of many things,
of love and hate,
laughter and tears...
of thoughts and emotions,
and young hearts' pure dreams.
Life is too short to be sad or unhappy
Too short to live only for self.
For the world and its pleasures
that last only for a time.
It takes just a moment...
a crash, then a scream...
A life and soul cast...
onto Eternity's shores.
As we live, so we die...
and it takes but one moment
to determine the direction we'll fall.
Just one moment... to pray,
"Dear God, forgive me."
Then a lifetime of happiness...
An Eternity in Heaven.
We so often think, it doesn't matter for today.
I'll repent tomorrow...
Today, I'll live my way.
Tomorrow never comes...
And maybe "your" eternity,
will begin suddenly... today.
Today. Before you took that one moment
to repent...
and be forgiven.
Oh, traveler along this pathway of life,
don't put off until tomorrow
what you can do today.
Tomorrow... never comes.
Your entrance into Eternity
may come Today.

Fleeting Moments

Fleeting moments that pass the screen of our eyes,
Fleeting, the pleasures of sin that we prize.
Glimpses of Heaven and the Father often lie in the past,
Our focus is on the things of earth that don't last.

The music that booms, assaulting our ears,
The billboard on the highway causing our eyes to veer...
The cell phone we carry can be sin's fire in our hand,
Growing bigger and hotter each time it is fanned.

A magazine we flip through is the devil's bait.
Even on a colorful dinner menu, temptations await.
Department store racks are bold and indecent, igniting desires...
That flame into grave sins, leading to hell's fires.

The beautiful lights of a casino beckon us in,
With the promise of big money: "Maybe this time you'll win!"
Then there's the bottle shop: "Let's just have one drink!"
Thereby some are addicted in the space of a blink.

Spiraling down, ever downward, "one drink at a time,"
Until they lose it all and slip into a life of crime.
Then alone, in a stupor, scrolling on the screen of their mind...
Replay pictures of a home, health, and loved family ties.

And the fleeting pleasures thought to be such a prize,
Are only bad memories and questions: "Why?"
Assaulted on every side by the devil's din,
If only we'd asked Jesus for His help to win!

Then those moments of earth that we held so dear
May have faded away into a different sphere...
And the life that we lived would be happy and free,
'Cause our eyes focus on Jesus... who died for you ... and me.

The Devil's Chains

What will it be like to stand on the brink
Of that flame-filled pit, full of devils black as ink...
To hear the hideous roaring, smell the sulfurous flame,
And feel the hate-filled cackles as they call your name?

"It's your turn," they'll scream as they push you in.
You'll pay forever... you chose your sin.
The first drink you took... then we tempted you with another,
And while you were driving drunk, you hit and killed someone's mother.

Then we invented syringes and pills, guaranteed to keep you high,
We made sure you were hooked with only one try...
Then you took your young women and sold them as slaves
To men with big money, so twisted and depraved.

We taught you to be thieves, to rape and kill.
To take someone's life for a trinket gave you a devilish thrill.
We whispered in your ear, "You don't need to tell the truth..."
And started you young, almost before you had a tooth.

Then we slunk in between a husband and wife,
Even though you promised to cherish each other for life.
We beguiled you to cheat; you began to squabble and shout.
Soon your home was broken with the children shoved about.

So we taught you anger, disrespect, and greed...
To hurt someone else seemed to fill some heart's need.
And families without love are just what we aimed for
Turning everyone we could away from Heaven's door.

Then we provoked you to lust, woman to woman, and man to man,
Dishonoring your own bodies, far away from God's plan.
When you're filled with disease, convinced you're destined for hell...
We devils know that we've won; we have done our job well.

Meanwhile, God, in His Infinite mercy from Above,
Continues to knock at your heart's door with such love.
He knocks and again... then so sadly turns away,
As He hopes that you'll open that door someday!

He watches from Heaven as your life falls apart,
Because of the sin you've allowed in your heart.
You're His prodigal child, bound by the devil's chains...
And He longs to unlock them and wash your heart's stains.

As long as you live, He'll be watching for you...
Always longing and waiting, your eternal home in view.
His Son's blood covers every stain that you wear.
He has a new robe of white that He'll give to you there.

Don't leave it too late; don't let the devil win,
Kneel down and ask God to forgive all your sin.
And the devils that have tempted you will turn away in defeat...
As you lay your will at the Master's feet.

"Wherefore God also gave them up to uncleanness
Through the lusts of their own hearts,
To dishonor their own bodies between themselves:
Who changed the truth of God into a lie, and worshipped and served
the creature more than the Creator, who is blessed forever. Amen.
For this cause God gave them up until vile affections:
for even their women did change the natural use
into that which is against nature:
And likewise also the men, leaving the natural use of the woman,
burned in their lust one toward another: men with men working that
which is unseemly and receiving in themselves that recompense
of their error which was meet."

— *Romans 1:24-27 KJV*

One Last Call

He called me from the depths of degrading sin
But I put Him off for an hour or two.
He asked me to sing someone's favorite hymn...
And I was unwilling, my mood too blue.

He asked me to visit a young man in jail
But instead, I sat down to read a book.
He nudged me to send a letter in the mail.
I couldn't be bothered... I had to cook.

He asked me to help teach in His Bible school
But I had to plant a garden and mow the lawn.
He asked me to live more of the Golden Rule...
When I became willing, my chance was gone.

He asked me to spend an extra hour in prayer
But I didn't have time to get on my knees.
My sister's deathly ill and He sent me there...
Still, I could not but my selfish self please.

He called for missionaries to heathen lands
But my time was full with family and friends.
He asked me to humble my heart 'neath His hand...
I heeded not, though my life's near the end.

His call knocked at my heart, and the preacher spoke,
But I turned deaf ears to the Spirit's power.
He called me! He called me! How 'twas my life wrote?
Finally... I heeded, in life's last hour.

I lay on my deathbed, my body old and worn,
Broken by years spent in sinful living.
I lay alone thinking, fear filling my form...
Hell's flames creeping close, Satan's imps tormenting.

Then Jesus came calling, calling so softly
With the promise of Peace and torments ending.
My heart now softened; I pleaded His mercy...
He forgave me, my sentence suspending.

Oh now I have gained my last hope and chance
He sent me my very last call...
If I could live o'er my sin blackened life
I'd serve Him... my heart, soul, and all.

Musings of a King

What are the duties that I face today?
They run through my mind as on my restless bed I lay...
How many shekels of gold will they need for gilding
The walls of the temple my people are building?

Gotta meet with the chef about my banquet tonight,
And see if my troops are all ready to fight.
Are they provisioned enough for a month-long campaign...
And coffins ready for all the soldiers who are slain?

I've got to sit on my throne for hours today.
What about two mothers fighting over one little babe?
And the shepherd's sheep straying into the neighbor's field...
They're squabbling about damage to the farmer's wheat yield.

Whose turn is it tonight to come to my bed?
I want to snack on new wine and freshly baked bread.
The fires need to be stoked, a warm blanket or two...
And windows wide open so the stars we can view.

Sometime during the day, I want to see my own boys.
Are they doing good in school? Do they have enough toys?
Do the girls have some pearls to adorn their hair...
Are their closets full of pretty robes to wear?

Is my accountant still honest? Are the priests still holy?
Have my servants been helping the blind, lame, and lowly?
Which temple will we worship at on the next holy day?
Which God and which wife? They've led me astray!

Now as I lie on my piercing bed of regrets,
I wish I could find a way to forget...
All the times that I've worshiped a different thing
Than the great God of Heaven, who anointed me King!

The Courtroom of the Ages

In the courtroom of the ages stands a man condemned to die
With the devil as the lawyer telling every kind of lie.
The scales of justice standing on a table near the door,
But the advocate for mercy, at the moment, has the floor.

As the lawyer shouts the charges and they pile up on the scale,
With just one word from Jesus, the lawyer's face begins to pale!
"The accused has asked for mercy, for his soul, my blood was shed..."
And the scales of justice balance when weighed by the flow of red.

Then the door of mercy opens and forgiven he walks out,
And the angels waiting welcome with a mighty ringing shout.
Now the devil brings the next one, cringing to the judgment bar,
There he stands accused and silent. Instead of God, he loved his car.

And the lawyer cackles grimly as he sends him out the door,
Into the clutches of his minions, who receive him with a roar.
Then he screams to the judge for mercy, but he's left it all too late,
And the imps of hell all drag him toward the fire, which is his fate.

One by one we'll pass before Him who sits upon the Throne.
With no one to stand there with us, we will face Him all alone.
And the sins that we've committed, written for the world to see,
Can be covered by the blood Jesus shed on Calvary's tree.

But our plea must be for mercy before we reach our day in court,
Or the scales that weigh our balance will be just a bit too short.
Oh don't wait until you face it with the devil waiting there,
To drag you with his demons into his fiery lair.

One Drop of Water

I woke in the morning, my throat parched and dry
As I reached for my water, there was one drop left inside.
It slid down my throat, still leaving a desert behind...
And for the relief of a full glass, I desperately pined.

So the rich man in the Bible begged for one drop to sate
The flames of his torment, the beggar who laid at his gate.
And in agony, he pled for someone his brothers to warn...
But Moses and the prophets, they continued to scorn.

So will we in our darkness, if we turn not to the light
Beg and scream for one drop to relieve our burning plight.
And there stands our Saviour, blood dripping to His feet...
Knocking, tirelessly knocking, hoping to lift our sin's defeat.

Slowly, so broken, He sorrowfully turns away.
Once again we've refused His offer, our debt to pay!
With leaden steps, He turns His back, a tear slips from His eye...
Instead of Heaven's wonders, we've chosen hell's flames leaping high.

There's a great gulf fixed between, it will forever keep you from the well
Of cool living water that would relieve your hell!
Don't refuse Him now, watching, as He dejectedly walks away...
For you'll wish to hear Him knocking, asking entrance again, someday!

"There was a certain rich man,
which was clothed in purple and fine linen,
and fared sumptuously every day:
And there was a certain beggar named Lazarus,
which was laid at his gate, full of sores,
And desiring to be fed with the crumbs
which fell from the rich man's table:
moreover the dogs came and licked his sores.
And it came to pass, that the beggar died,
and was carried by the angels into Abraham's bosom:
the rich man also died, and was buried;
And in hell he lift up his eyes, being in torments,
and seeth Abraham afar off, and Lazarus in his bosom.
And he cried and said, Father Abraham, have mercy on me,
and send Lazarus, that he may dip the tip of his finger in water,
and cool my tongue; for I am tormented in this flame.
But Abraham said, Son, remember that thou in thy lifetime
receivedst thy good things, and likewise Lazarus evil things:
but now he is comforted, and thou art tormented.
And beside all this, between us and you there is a great gulf fixed:
so that they which would pass from hence to you cannot;
neither can they pass to us, that would come from thence.
Then he said, I pray thee therefore, father,
that thou wouldest send him to my father's house:
For I have five brethren; that he may testify unto them,
lest they also come into this place of torment.
Abraham saith unto him, They have Moses and the prophets;
let them hear them. And he said, Nay, father Abraham:
but if one went unto them from the dead, they will repent.
And he said unto him, If they hear not Moses and the prophets,
neither will they be persuaded, though one rose from the dead."

— *Luke 16:19-31 KJV*

The Locked Door

In the cold and snowy, windy winter's night
Locked out in the darkness with no one in sight...
As I knocked and knocked, not a soul seemed to hear,
No coat... no key... beginning to freeze, I fear.

So as I knocked some more, I sent a prayer winging high
Hoping the line between us was open, and He would reply.
Undeserving though I am, He answered my prayer.
Not a minute later, suddenly, my husband was there.

In a meeting, a voice whispered, "Go check on your wife."
And he listened, came looking. I went in to warm life.
I knew that the line to the Father above
Was open and pulsing with His Infinite Love.

And the door that was locked when I tried to go in
The Lord locked to teach me, I needed to trust Him...
That He listens when I pray, and answers in His time.
As I keep communication open, I feel the tug on the line.

So when it's my turn to knock on the Heavenly gate,
I pray that I'll never be locked out or too late.
Turned away from that door, sentenced to hell,
Because I failed to heed the Father's warning bell.

Locked away forever from that beautiful place,
Sent to the regions where the devil has space.
Burning and burning, never an end to the flames...
Forever reviewing each sin in our name.

In The Fog

When the fog comes drifting, tendrils creeping o'er the land,
And misty droplets cling to every leaf and tree that stand...
It settles in slowly and deepens in the night,
'Til you can't see where to go or which way is right.

It thickens and deadens the sound in the air,
And everything is enclosed in its silvery hair.
The tendrils swirl and dance in the breeze's song...
As the night grows deeper and darker and long.

So the fog of our sin begins to deaden our hearts,
As we dabble a bit; we're soon led apart...
The devil tells us we're alone, and we're deafened by the din,
And the night 'round us deepens, shrouded by sin.

As the fog cuts off our sight to the pathway ahead,
So the chains of sin bind us as if weighted with lead...
As they wind ever tighter, slowly life is choked out,
Then the devil lives in glee, he no longer has to doubt.

That he's won you to his side, leaving God behind,
And he continues to lie and sin's chains to wind...
And the heart once soft and led by God's Hand,
Is hard and cold. No embers left to be fanned.

And still the Lord in His love and infinite kindness
Shines His light, again and again, hoping to lift the blindness.
And dispel the fog and ever-darkening despair...
Into the light of His Son on the wings of a prayer.

The Ship of Grace

There's a ship anchored in blue water, fathoms deep,
Gently rocking on the waves with their endless sweep.
Its bulwarks shine bright, seen from a faraway place,
And the flag flying on the flagstaff reads, "His Majesty's Ship: Grace."

Its holystoned decks glisten, the cables coiled bow and stern,
The infirmary stocked with supplies for injuries or rope burn.
All the galley shelves filled, everything a chef might need,
To create beautiful tasty feasts and the hungry crowd feed.

Lifeboats line the rails, emergency rations stored in place,
And life jackets and flares each take up some space.
The life preservers are hung on the side close at hand,
For the crew to throw out to a drowning man.

The Captain stands by the rail, endlessly scanning the sea,
Anxiously looking for shipwrecks, like you and me.
Cracked up on rocks, hidden under the waves,
But He stands there on guard, His precious souls to save.

And when someone is spotted going under once, and again...
His crew jumps to His cry, "There's a drowning man!"
Then the lifeline is thrown out, all the crew standing by,
Ready to reel in the line, e'er the man dies.

And the man in the water reaching for the line,
Must let go of his driftwood raft and try one more time.
With faith that he'll catch it, and be drawn into the "Grace."
Where there's safety and love in the Captain's face.

With every care for those saved, the Captain still scans for the lost,
And He paid for your passage at tremendous cost.
He patiently stands waiting and lovingly beckons you in...
And when you reach up in faith, His Grace forgives your sin.

So your ship of Grace steams on with room to spare,
And you must tell others this wonderful Grace is there.
Now you work for the Captain. You are on His crew,
Ready to throw out the lifeline, someone's faith to renew.

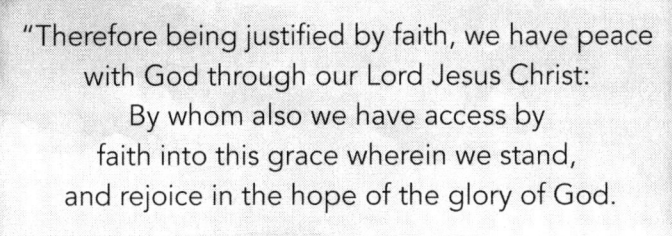

"Therefore being justified by faith, we have peace
with God through our Lord Jesus Christ:
By whom also we have access by
faith into this grace wherein we stand,
and rejoice in the hope of the glory of God.

— **Romans 5:1-2 KJV**

Acknowledgements

To all whom I have met along this journey toward home

Family, friends, strangers
Preachers and teachers,

All who have touched my life
Leaving impressions and touches of yourself...

I count each a treasure,
And from these jewels
Comes inspiration
From our Heavenly Father!

About the Author

THE SOUND OF BIRDS SINGING... an endless sunset from a window seat... times of joy and times of shattering grief... scripture... a song or sermon... the words of a child or a friend... these are the kinds of moments that inspire Beth Sundberg to write a poem.

As a tender woman, barely 20 years old, Beth left the family farm in Louisiana's bayous for a destiny in the snowy lands of North Dakota in the early 80s. She wrote her first poem, "Thanks for a Smile to Share," (page 44) while teaching school in the new and foreign terrain. There she met a handsome farmer and together they built a family and a home.

Since that first poem, Beth has kept a notebook close by to capture the lines and stanzas of her life as a Christian, farmer's wife, mother, grandmother, daughter, sister, aunt, cousin, friend, and very busy caterer.

In more than forty years, she has written nearly two hundred poems. Until publishing *The Artist's Canvas*, most had never been seen by anyone outside family or close friends.

Beth and her husband live in a home by a river in North Dakota. Besides the river, the view from her windows includes fields of crops and an arboretum of brilliantly-colored trees planted carefully by her husband.

When she's not writing poems, Beth enjoys cooking – *which is a good thing since she does so much of it!* – as well as reading, sewing quilt tops, spending time with her family, especially her grandchildren, traveling, and singing.

Since her new birth conversion as a young person, Beth has been a devoted member of the Church of God in Christ, Mennonite. She has tremendous faith that God hears and answers prayer. Her fervent desire is that people who read her poems will see Jesus and love Him because He loves us so!

There's More!
Find The Artist's Canvas, Book One, on Amazon.com